DINOSAURS

CONTENTS

Life on Earth. 5
Just Before the Dinosaurs 6
The First Dinosaurs. 8
The Meat Eaters 10
The Biggest Dinosaurs 12
Other Long-Necked Dinosaurs . . 14
The Bird-Footed Dinosaurs. 16
Foldout: 150 Million Years Ago 19
Other Bird-Footed Dinosaurs . . . 24
The Plated Dinosaurs 26
The Ankylosaurs 28
The Horned Dinosaurs 30
Dinosaur Babies 32
Other Prehistoric Reptiles 33
After the Dinosaurs. 34
Amazing Dinosaur Facts 36
Glossary 37
Index. 38

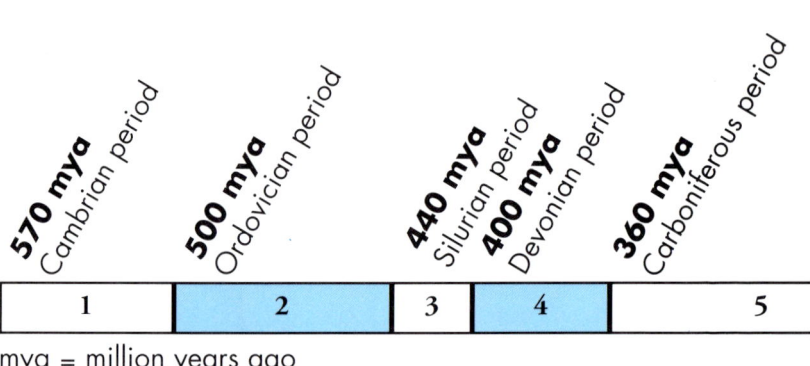

570 mya Cambrian period
500 mya Ordovician period
440 mya Silurian period
400 mya Devonian period
360 mya Carboniferous period

| 1 | 2 | 3 | 4 | 5 |

mya = million years ago

LIFE ON EARTH

Scientists study rocks and fossils to learn about Earth's past. During different geological **periods**, spanning millions of years, different plants and animals **evolved** and died out. The first primitive life forms – algae, worms, and jellyfish – arose in the Precambrian period, 4 billion years ago.

A GEOLOGICAL TIMESCALE	
1 **Cambrian period**	Primitive invertebrates live in the seas.
2 **Ordovician period**	Early fish appear.
3 **Silurian period**	Land plants and insects appear.
4 **Devonian period**	Amphibians appear.
5 **Carboniferous period**	First **reptiles** live in swampy forests.
6 **Permian period**	Archosaurs appear.
7 **Triassic period**	First **mammals** and dinosaurs evolve.
8 **Jurassic period**	Dinosaurs dominate.
9 **Cretaceous period**	Dinosaurs begin to dissappear.
10 **Tertiary period**	Most dinosaurs die. Mammals dominate.
11 **Quaternary period**	Humans appear.

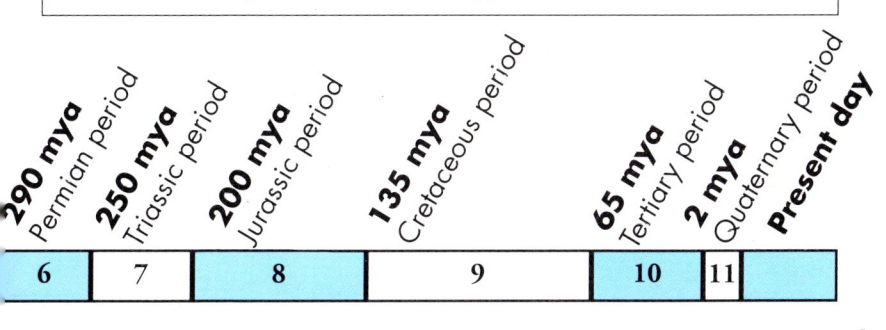

290 mya Permian period | **250 mya** Triassic period | **200 mya** Jurassic period | **135 mya** Cretaceous period | **65 mya** Tertiary period | **2 mya** Quaternary period | **Present day**

| 6 | 7 | 8 | 9 | 10 | 11 | |

JUST BEFORE THE DINOSAURS

During the late Permian period and early Triassic period, 290–250 million years ago, the dominant four-legged land animals were the early **synapsids**. Scientists believe that these ancient ancestors of modern **mammals** may have been **warm-blooded**.

Kannemeyeria
Kannemeyeria's teeth tell us that this synapsid ate plants.

Cynognathus
Cynognathus had the powerful jaws and sharp teeth of a meat eater.

Ericiolacerta
This small synapsid probably ate insects.

The archosaurs were another group of large four-legged animals that lived during the Triassic period. Crocodiles, flying reptiles, birds, and dinosaurs evolved from the archosaurs.

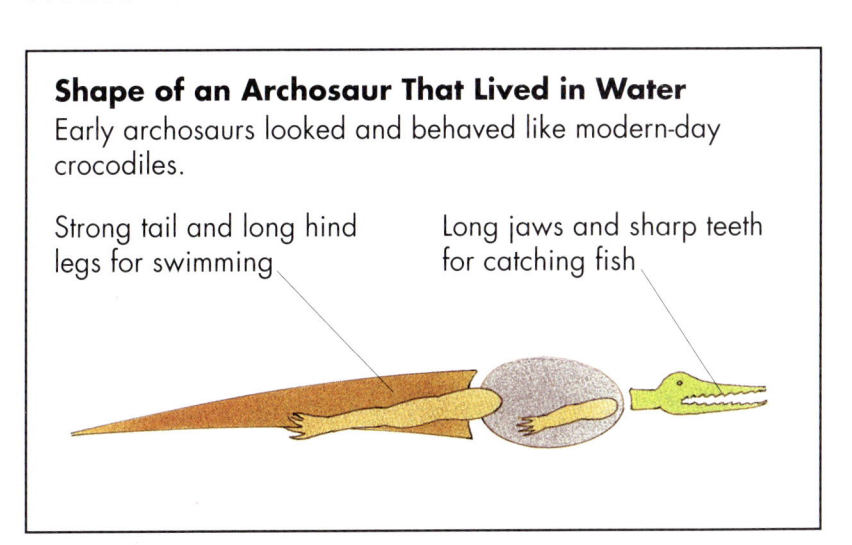

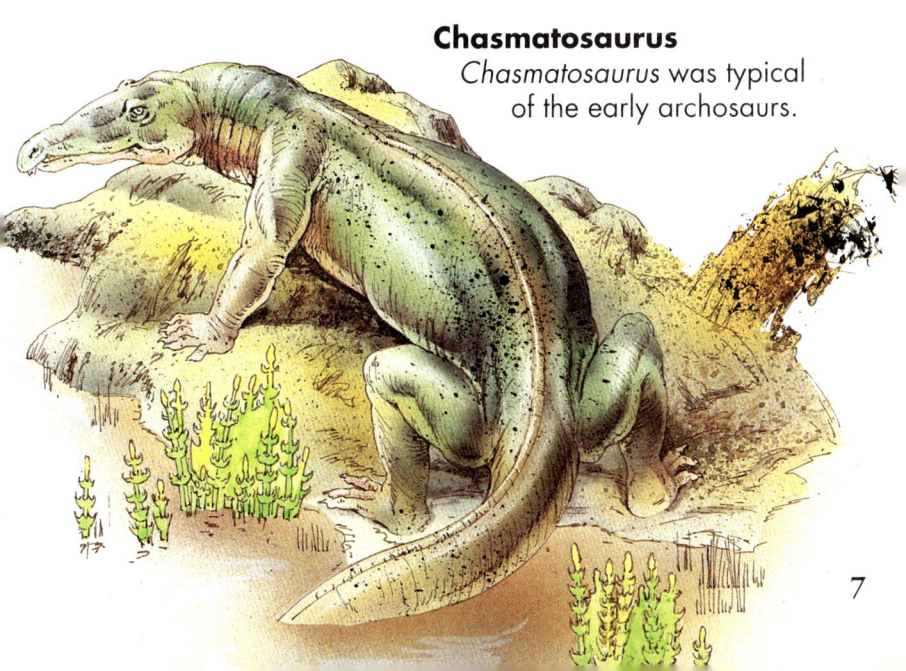

Shape of an Archosaur That Lived in Water
Early archosaurs looked and behaved like modern-day crocodiles.

Strong tail and long hind legs for swimming

Long jaws and sharp teeth for catching fish

Chasmatosaurus
Chasmatosaurus was typical of the early archosaurs.

7

THE FIRST DINOSAURS

No one knows why, but most of the synapsids died out at the end of the Triassic period. When one group of animals dies out, another group of animals takes over. At the end of the Triassic period, the archosaurs became the dominant four-legged animals.

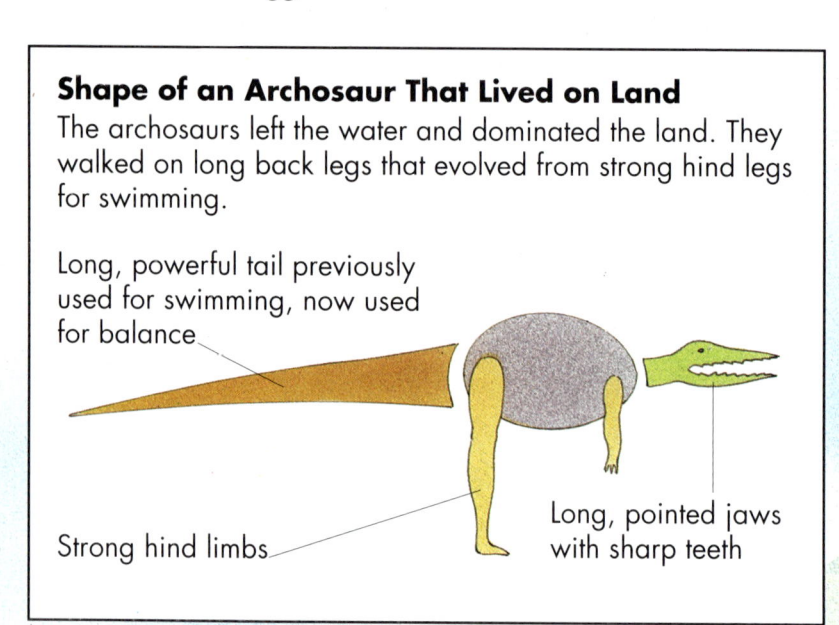

Shape of an Archosaur That Lived on Land
The archosaurs left the water and dominated the land. They walked on long back legs that evolved from strong hind legs for swimming.

Long, powerful tail previously used for swimming, now used for balance

Strong hind limbs

Long, pointed jaws with sharp teeth

Long jaws and sharp, meat-cutting teeth

Short forelimbs with sharp claws to catch **prey**

Herrerasaurus

Herrerasaurus was one of the earliest dinosaurs. Like later dinosaurs, it had a more upright stance than early archosaurs.

A long, heavy tail helped balance the whole body.

Strong hind legs for running

THE MEAT EATERS

Hundreds of different kinds of dinosaurs evolved in the Triassic, Jurassic, and Cretaceous periods. One group is the **theropods**, also known as the meat eaters. Theropods came in various shapes and sizes. Many had sharp teeth and long hind legs and tails like *Herrerasaurus* and early archosaurs.

Tyrannosaurus
One of the biggest meat eaters, *Tyrannosaurus*, was 40 feet long. Its seven-inch teeth were razor-sharp!

Compsognathus
The smallest known dinosaur was about the size of a chicken.

Dromiceiomimus
This fast runner looked like an ostrich.

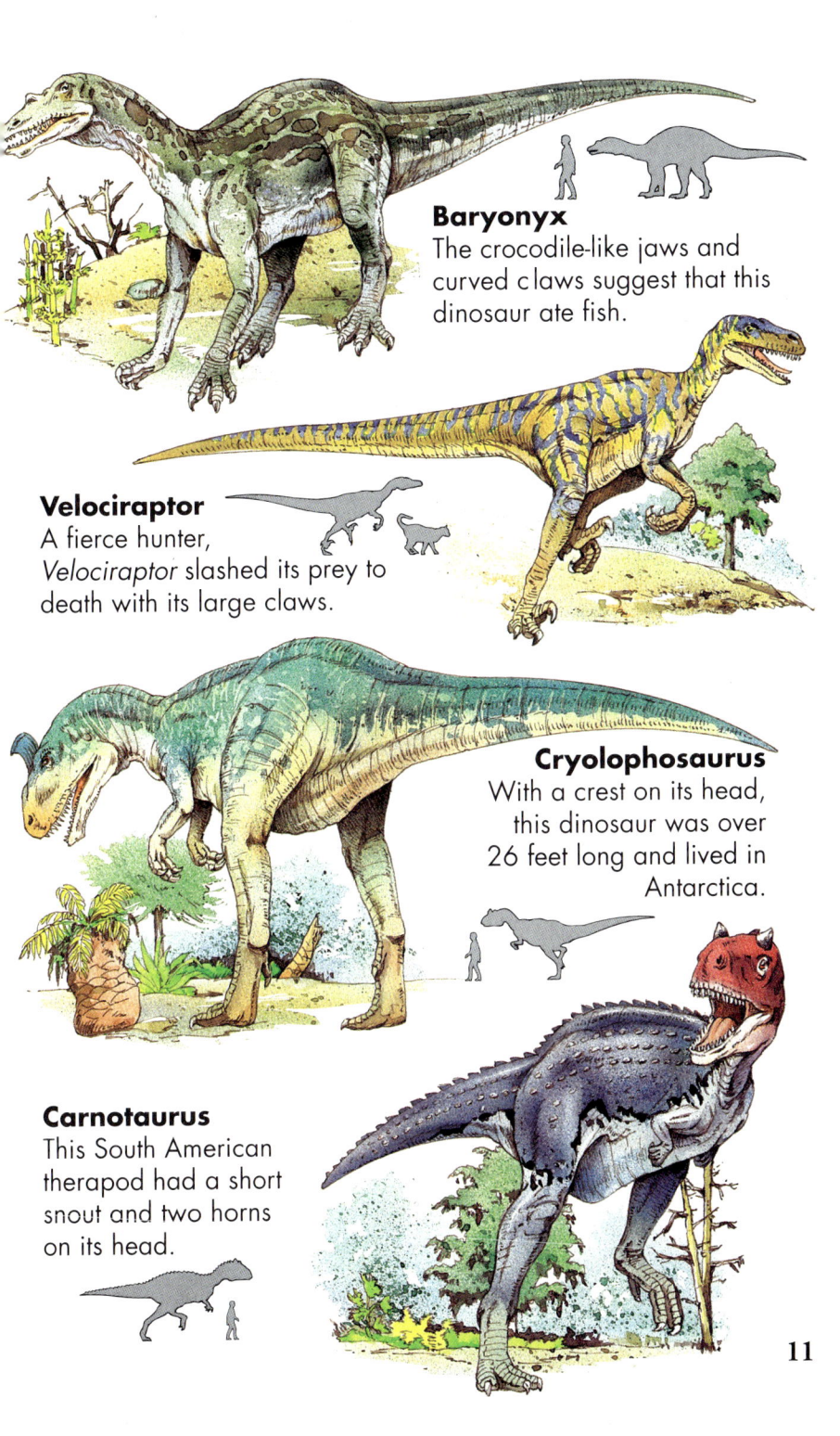

Baryonyx
The crocodile-like jaws and curved claws suggest that this dinosaur ate fish.

Velociraptor
A fierce hunter, *Velociraptor* slashed its prey to death with its large claws.

Cryolophosaurus
With a crest on its head, this dinosaur was over 26 feet long and lived in Antarctica.

Carnotaurus
This South American therapod had a short snout and two horns on its head.

11

THE BIGGEST DINOSAURS

The largest creatures ever to walk on Earth were the long-necked plant eaters. Scientists call them **sauropods**. Many scientists believe that sauropods developed long necks to help them reach the leaves at the tops of tall trees. Sauropods had large torsos to hold the large **digestive systems** needed to break down plant material.

Seismosaurus

The biggest sauropod was *Seismosaurus*. It was about 130 feet long. Its neck was twice as long as a bus!

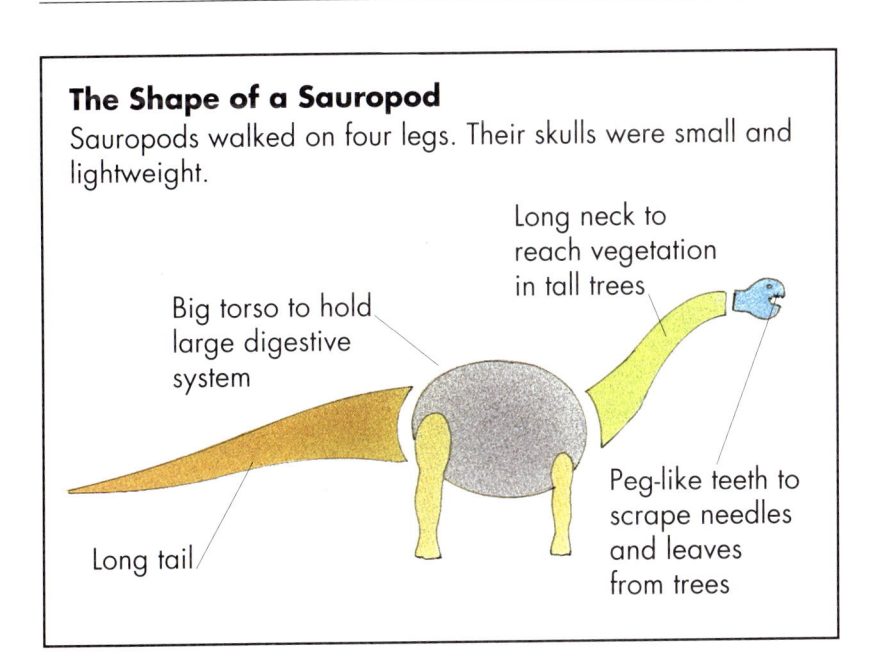

The Shape of a Sauropod
Sauropods walked on four legs. Their skulls were small and lightweight.

Long neck to reach vegetation in tall trees

Big torso to hold large digestive system

Peg-like teeth to scrape needles and leaves from trees

Long tail

Seismosaurus and other sauropods had long tails that they held up for balance as they walked.

Seismosaurus must have weighed 100 tons, as much as 15 elephants.

OTHER LONG-NECKED DINOSAURS

All sauropods ate plants. Scientists believe sauropods scraped leaves off trees and swallowed them unchewed. Then they swallowed stones to crush the leaves in their stomachs.

Amargasaurus
This South American sauropod had spikes and frills down its neck and back.

Saltasaurus
Also from South America, this sauropod had unusual armor.

Shunosaurus
Common in China, this dinosaur had a club at the end of its tail.

14

Mamenchisaurus
This sauropod's 36-foot neck was the longest neck of any dinosaur!

Brachiosaurus
High shoulders and a long neck enabled *Brachiosaurus* to feed on tall trees.

Diplodocus
This dinosaur stood up on its hind legs to reach leaves.

THE BIRD-FOOTED DINOSAURS

Ornithopods were the bird-footed dinosaurs. All ornithopods were plant eaters. They had strong hind legs and three-toed feet that resembled birds' feet. They also had beaks, cheek pouches, and teeth designed for crushing and grinding leaves and pine needles. Some ornithopods had large crests on the top of their heads.

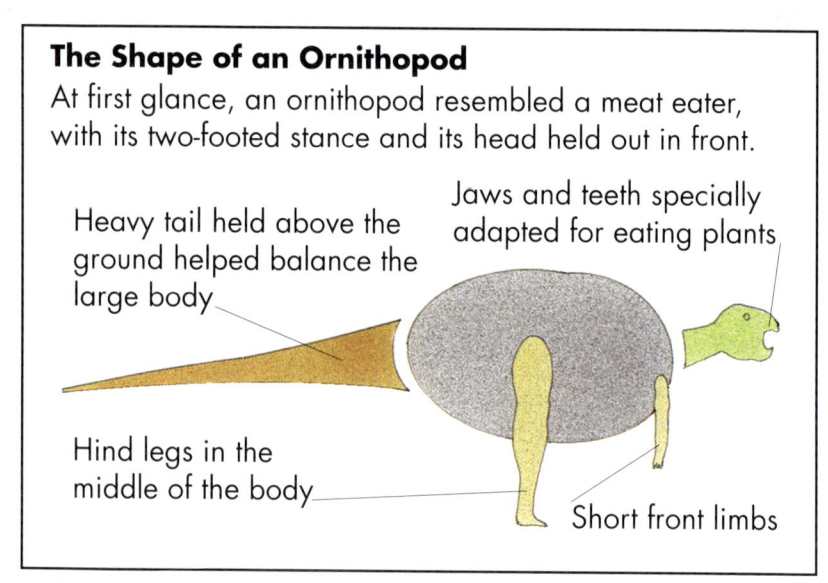

The Shape of an Ornithopod
At first glance, an ornithopod resembled a meat eater, with its two-footed stance and its head held out in front.

Heavy tail held above the ground helped balance the large body

Jaws and teeth specially adapted for eating plants

Hind legs in the middle of the body

Short front limbs

What did they eat?
Ornithopods ate the leaves and needles of cycads, ferns, ginkgo, and yew trees. They held food in their cheek pouches while they chewed.

The ornithopods ranged in size from that of cats to that of small trucks. Over thirty feet long, *Iguanodon* was the largest ornithopod. *Iguanodon* was also the first dinosaur ever discovered. It was found in England in 1822. The name *Iguanodon* comes from the Spanish word "iguana" and the Greek word "odon"(tooth). Its teeth are similar to those of a modern iguana.

Iguanodon

All ornithopods had beaks.

Walking
Although they were two-footed, some of the bigger ornithopods may have also walked on four legs.

Bird-Footed
Their three-toed feet were similar to those of birds.

A DINOSAUR SITE TODAY

Scientists learn about dinosaurs by studying their bones and other **fossils** found in rocks. The fossils of many different dinosaurs from the Jurassic period were found on a hillside near the Colorado-Utah border in 1909. The site is now Dinosaur National Monument.

Stegosaurus plates

Apatosaurus bones

Crocodile bone

Camarasaurus skeleton

Fossil trunk of a conifer tree

Allosaurus skeleton

Comodactylus
(Pterosaur)

Camarasaurus

Stegosaurus

Phascolodon
(Early mammal)

Goniopholis (Crocodile)

150 MILLION YEARS AGO

During the Jurassic period, the area now known as Dinosaur National Monument might have looked like this. Redwood, ginkgo, and monkey puzzle trees grew in forests. Long-necked plant eaters fed on these trees, ferns, and other plants. Meat eaters hunted other dinosaurs. The bones of dead dinosaurs sank into the sand and mud. Over millions of years, the sand and mud became rocks and the bones turned into fossils.

Allosaurus

OTHER BIRD-FOOTED DINOSAURS

The ornithopods were very successful. By the end of the Cretaceous period, they were the most widespread and numerous plant eaters.

Ouranosaurus
This 23-foot-long dinosaur with a fin down its back lived in Africa.

Pachycephalosaurus
The lump of bone on its head was used as a battering ram.

Hadrosaurus
One of the biggest plant eaters.

Parasaurolophus
This duck-billed ornithopod had a six-foot hollow crest on its head.

One group of ornithopods, the hadrosaurs, or duck-billed dinosaurs, often had crests on their heads. Scientists believe that the crests may have been used to make trumpet or flutelike sounds.

Some small ornithopods, like *Hypsilophodon* and *Lesothosaurus*, were fast runners and may have reached speeds of up to thirty miles per hour! Their size and speed probably helped them escape from predators.

Hypsilophodon
With its long, slender hind legs, this plant eater was a very fast runner.

Lesothosaurus
This early plant eater lacked the cheek pouches that the later ornithopods developed.

25

THE PLATED DINOSAURS

Some dinosaurs had protective armor. One group of armored dinosaurs, the **stegosaurs**, had small pieces of bone in the skin of their necks and spikes on their tails. Some also had tall plates down their backs. These heavy dinosaurs ate plants and walked on four legs.

The Shape of a Stegosaur
Stegosaurs varied in size, but they all had small heads and tiny brains. The double row of plates on their backs may have been used as armor or like **solar panels**, absorbing the heat of the sun to warm the stegosaur's body.

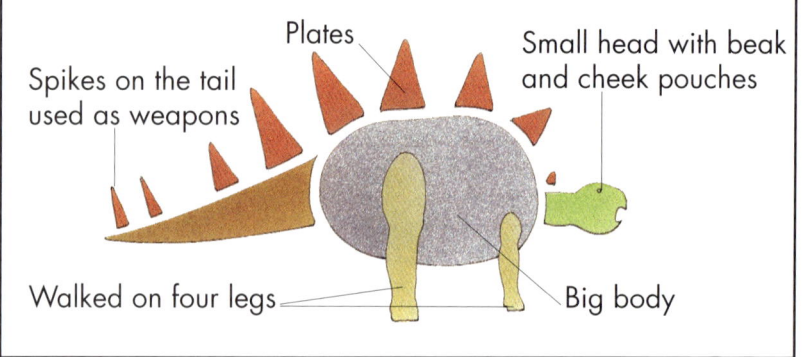

Plates

Small head with beak and cheek pouches

Spikes on the tail used as weapons

Walked on four legs

Big body

Yangshanosaurus
This Chinese stegosaur had huge shoulder spines.

Stegosaurus
Found in western North America, the brain of Stegosaurus was only the size of a walnut.

Lexovisaurus
This European stegosaur had narrow plates and spines.

Tuojiangosaurus
Rows of small triangular plates lined the back of this Chinese stegosaur.

Wuerhosaurus
The plates of this Chinese stegosaur were long and low.

THE ANKYLOSAURS

Another group of armored dinosaurs were the **ankylosaurs**. They had bony armor under the skin of their backs and tails, and their skulls were thick and strong. When attacked by large meat-eating dinosaurs, ankylosaurs crouched close to the ground, letting their armored skin protect them.

The Shape of an Ankylosaur
Heavy armor was set into the skin of the ankylosaur's back. Many had bony clubs at the ends of their tails. Their heads were also heavily armored. Some even had bony armor on their eyelids!

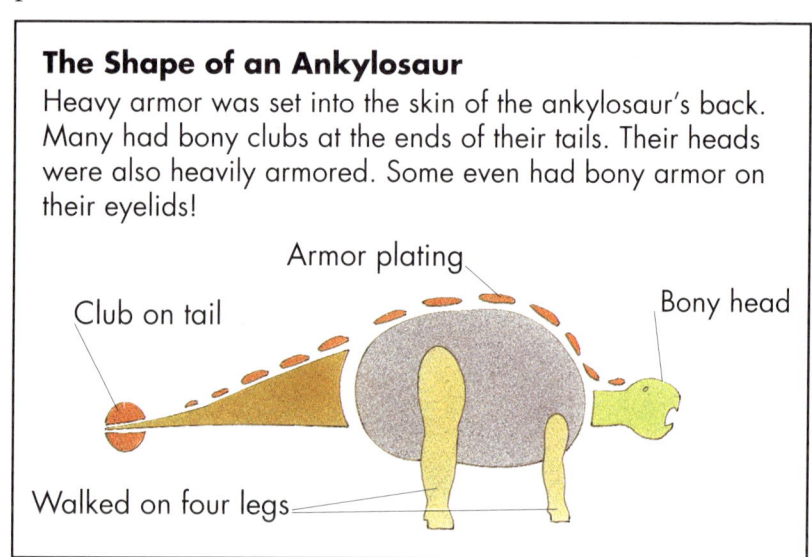

- Armor plating
- Club on tail
- Bony head
- Walked on four legs

Euoplocephalus
Even though heavy armor plates covered its neck and back, this ankylosaur was surprisingly agile.

Scelidosaurus
This cow-sized species is the earliest known example of an armored dinosaur.

Struthiosaurus
Struthiosaurus lived in Europe. It was about the size of a sheep.

Mymoorapelta
This ankylosaur had spines on its sides and blades on its tail.

Ankylosaurus
The last and largest of the ankylosaurs was up to 30 feet long and lived in North America.

THE HORNED DINOSAURS

Triceratops and its relatives belong to the group called **ceratopsians**. All ceratopsians had bony frills on the backs of their heads. Most, though not all, had horns over their eyes and on their snouts. Ceratopsian fossils have been found together in large groups, which suggests they may have traveled in herds.

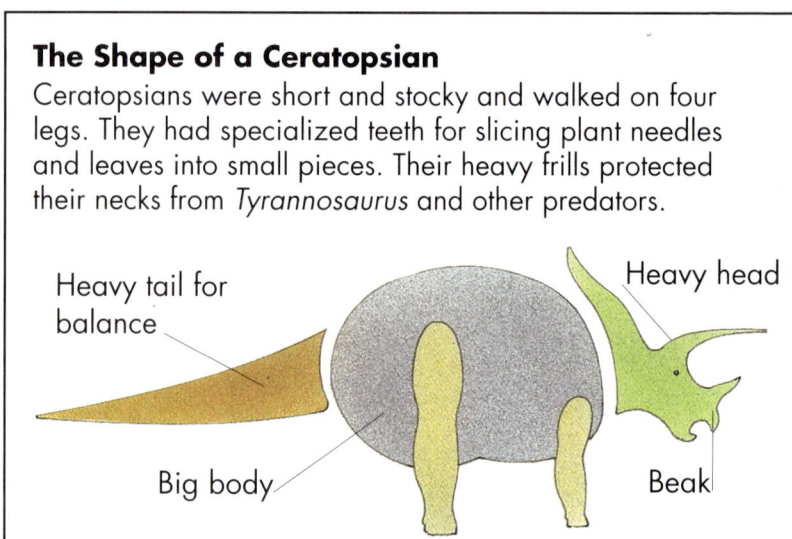

The Shape of a Ceratopsian
Ceratopsians were short and stocky and walked on four legs. They had specialized teeth for slicing plant needles and leaves into small pieces. Their heavy frills protected their necks from *Tyrannosaurus* and other predators.

Heavy tail for balance

Heavy head

Big body

Beak

Triceratops
The biggest of the horned dinosaurs, *Triceratops* was about 30 feet long. It had one horn on its snout and two over its eyes.

Styracosaurus
Spikes surrounded the neck frill of *Styracosaurus*. It also had an enormous horn on its snout.

Chasmosaurus
Chasmosaurus had the largest frill of all the ceratopsians.

Pachyrhinosaurus
Pachyrhinosaurus had a solid battering ram instead of a horn.

Einiosaurus
The horn on *Einiosaurus* turned downward. It also had two spikes at the top of its frill.

Diceratops
Diceratops was similar to *Triceratops* but did not have a horn on its snout.

DINOSAUR BABIES

Like modern birds and reptiles, dinosaurs probably laid hard-shelled eggs in nests. The eggs of many different kinds of dinosaurs have been found, some containing skeletons. Whole nests have also been discovered containing the fossils of baby dinosaurs, with the remains of parent dinosaurs nearby. These nests tell scientists how dinosaurs raised their young.

Nests containing fossilized eggs and young of the duck-billed dinosaur *Maiasaura* were found in Montana.

The teeth of the baby *Maiasaura* were worn. This suggests that their parents brought food back to the nest.

The remains of the young *Maiasaura* found near the nests were of different sizes, indicating that young dinosaurs may have stayed with their parents for several years.

OTHER PREHISTORIC REPTILES

Dinosaurs were not the only animals living during the Triassic, Jurassic, and Cretaceous periods. Flying reptiles, called pterosaurs, soared through the air. Some were the size of small airplanes! Large marine reptiles, like plesiosaurs, pliosaurs, and ichthyosaurs, ruled the oceans.

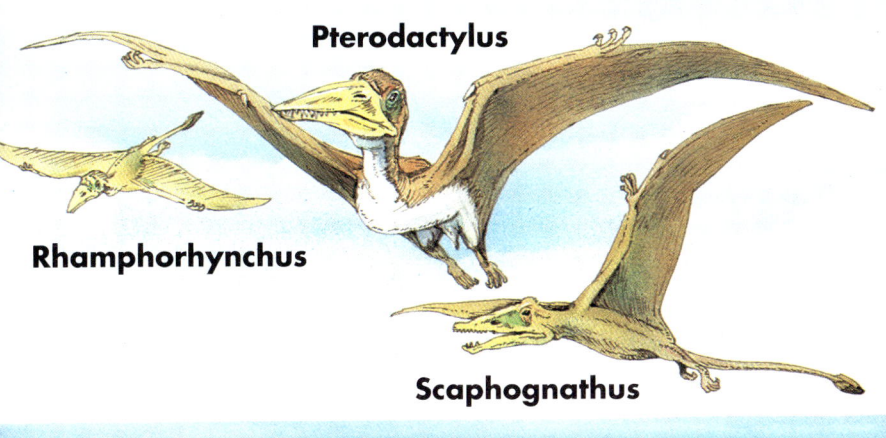

Pterodactylus

Rhamphorhynchus

Scaphognathus

Plesiosaur

Marine Reptiles
Plesiosaurs, pliosaurs, and ichthyosaurs had streamlined bodies for swimming.

Pliosaur

Ichthyosaur

AFTER THE DINOSAURS

At the end of the Cretaceous period, the dinosaurs and the flying and swimming reptiles suddenly died out. Scientists do not know why. The many theories include a massive meteorite hitting Earth or a dramatic climate change caused by a catastrophic volcanic eruption.

Early Mammals

Icaronycteris
Early bats like *Icaronycteris* replaced pterosaurs.

Uintatherium
Rhino-like mammals replaced large plant-eating dinosaurs.

Hyaenodon
Carnivorous mammals replaced meat-eating dinosaurs.

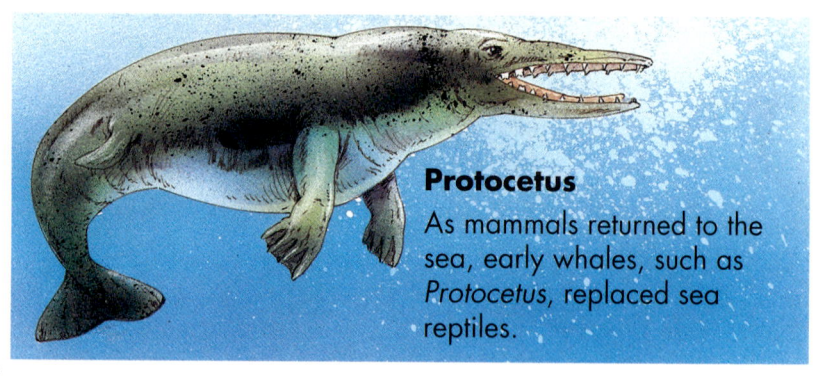

Protocetus
As mammals returned to the sea, early whales, such as *Protocetus*, replaced sea reptiles.

As the dinosaurs died out during the Tertiary period, mammals became the dominant four-legged land creatures. Two million years ago, at the end of the Tertiary period, the first humans appeared.

Amebelodon
Early elephants were the largest plant eaters.

Megatylopus
Camels evolved as grassland replaced forests.

Osteoborus
Dogs and cats took over as the primary meat eaters.

Synthetoceras
Long-legged, long-faced **herbivores** roamed the grasslands.

Epigaulus
Early burrowing rodents fed on roots and underground stems.

AMAZING DINOSAUR FACTS

- **First discovery** The first recorded dinosaur remains were found in England in 1822 by Dr. Gideon Mantell. He named it *Iguanodon*. The name dinosaur means "terrible lizard" in Greek. It was first used by British naturalist Sir Richard Owen in 1841.

Einiosaurus

- **Einiosaurus** The down-turned horn of *Einiosaurus* is a puzzle to scientists. Some scientists believe the unusual angle of the horn may have been used to attract a mate.

- **Giganotosaurus** The skeleton of the largest meat eating dinosaur was found in 1995. *Giganotosaurus* lived in Patagonia, South America, 97 million years ago. It was 41 feet long and weighed almost 8 tons!

- **Biggest dig** The world's largest dinosaur dig took place in Tanzania, Africa, from 1907-1911. The world's biggest complete skeleton, of *Brachiosaurus*, was discovered there.

- **Living dinosaurs** Most scientists now agree that birds are actually living dinosaurs. One group of theropods, the maniraptors, are believed to be the ancestors of modern-day birds.

- **Diplodocus** This sauropod was over 87 feet long! Its tail alone had over 70 bones.

- **Longest name** The dinosaur with the longest name, *Micropachycephalosaurus*, was also one of the smallest. This ornithopod was only 20 inches long.

Diplodocus

GLOSSARY

Ankylosaur An armored dinosaur. The name means "fused reptile."

Archosaur A group that includes crocodiles, dinosaurs, and pterosaurs.

Carnivorous Meat-eating.

Ceratopsian A horned dinosaur. The name means "horned head."

Digestive system All the organs, such as the stomach, intestine, and alimentary canal, that are used by an animal for absorbing its food and extracting the nutrition.

Evolve To change gradually over the years, eventually developing into new species.

Fossil The remains of any once-living thing preserved in rock. A fossil may be a part of the original body, footprints, or burrows.

Herbivore A plant-eating animal.

Ichthyosaur A fish-shaped sea reptile that lived at the time of the dinosaurs.

Mammal A warm-blooded animal with hair or fur that bears live young and feeds them on mother's milk.

Ornithopod A group of plant-eating dinosaurs. The name means "bird-footed."

Period A stretch of time in Earth's history, usually millions of years, during which particular animals and plants existed.

Predator An animal that hunts and eats other animals.

Prey An animal that is hunted and eaten by another animal.

Reptile A cold-blooded, backboned animal with scaly skin that lays hard-shelled eggs on land.

Sauropod A long-necked plant eater. The name means "lizard-footed."

Solar panel A device that collects the energy of the sun and uses it to produce power or warmth.

Stegosaur A plated dinosaur. The name means "roofed reptile."

Synapsids A group of animals that lived just before the dinosaurs. They had mammal-like legs and mammal-like teeth.

Theropod A meat-eating dinosaur. The name means "beast-footed."

Warm-blooded An animal that makes its own body heat.

INDEX OF ILLUSTRATED DINOSAURS

A

Allosaurus 21
Amargasaurus 14
Amebelodon 35
Ankylosaurus 29
Apatasaurus 19, 20

B

Baryonyx 11
Brachiosaurus 15

C

Camarasaurus 22
Carnotaurus 11
Chasmatosaurus 7
Chasmosaurus 31
Comodactylus 22
Compsognathus 10
Cryolophosaurus 11
Cynognathus 6

D

Diceratops 31
Diplodocus 15, 36
Dromiceiomimus 10

E

Einiosaurus 31, 36
Epigaulus 35
Ericiolacerta 6
Euoplocephalus 28

G

Goniophalis 22

H

Hadrosaurus 24

Herrerasaurus 8, 9
Hyaenodon 34
Hypsilophodon 25

I

Icaronycterys 34
ichthyosaur 33
Iguanodon 17

K

Kannemeyeria 6

L

Lesothosaurus 25
Lexovisaurus 27

M

Maiasaura 32
Mamenchisaurus 15
Megatylopus 35
Mesadactylus 20
Mymoorapelta 29

O

Osteoborus 35
Ouranosaurus 24

P

Pachycephalosaurus 24
Pachyrhinosaurus 31
Parasaurolophus 24
Paramacellodus 19
Phascolodon 22
plesiosaur 33
pliosaur 33
Protocetus 34
Pterodactylus 33